CAPTURED
SCIENCE
HISTORY

TRASH VORTEX

HOW PLASTIC POLLUTION IS CHOKING THE WORLD'S OCEANS

by Danielle Smith-Llera

Content Adviser: Michael Wert, PhD
Associate Professor of History
Marquette University

COMPASS POINT BOOKS
a capstone imprint

Compass Point Books are published by Capstone,
1710 Roe Crest Drive, North Mankato, Minnesota 56003
www.mycapstone.com

Editor: Catherine Neitge
Designer: Catherine Neitge
Media Researcher: Svetlana Zhurkin
Library Consultant: Kathleen Baxter
Production Specialist: Laura Manthe

Image Credits
Alamy: Jonathan Plant, 47; Dreamstime: Andrew Sabai, 31; Getty Images: Bloomberg/
Jonathan Alcorn, 25, DPPI/Liot Vapillion, 53, *Los Angeles Times*/Al Seib, 55, Nature
Picture Library/Michael Pitts, cover, 33, Picture Post, 19, The LIFE Picture Collection/
Peter Stackpole, 23, WireImage/Don Arnold, 45; iStockphoto: negaprion, 41; Library
of Congress, 56 (top); NASA: JPL, 6–7; Newscom: akg-images, 17, Ambient Images/
Peter Bennett, 11, 13, 58 (bottom), MCT/Lyhne, 9, picture-alliance/dpa/Bodo Marks,
29, picture-alliance/dpa/Stefan Sauer, 27, Reuters/eurekalet/Oona Lonnstedt, 37,
Reuters/Tyrone Siu, 34, Zuma Press/J. Gerard Seguia, 51, Zuma Press/Jonathan
Alcorn, 5; Shutterstock: Africa Studio, 59, AuNging, 21, daizuoxin, 58 (top), De Jongh
Photography, 15, Don Mammoser, 43, Indonesiapix, 50, josefkubes, 56 (bottom),
neftali, 57, Oscar Espinosa, 39, Rawpixel, 49, Rich Carey, 30

Library of Congress Cataloging-in-Publication Data

Names: Smith-Llera, Danielle, 1971- author.
Title: Trash vortex : how plastic pollution is choking the world's oceans /
by Danielle Smith-Llera
Description: North Mankato, Minnesota : Capstone Press, [2018] | Series: CPB
grades 4-8. Captured science history | Includes bibliographical references and index. |
Audience: Age 10-14.
Identifiers: LCCN 2017037868 (print) | LCCN 2017038535 (ebook) | ISBN 9780756557539
(eBook PDF) | ISBN 9780756557454 (hardcover) | ISBN 9780756557492 (paperback)
Subjects: LCSH: Plastic marine debris—Environmental aspects—Juvenile literature. |
Marine pollution—Juvenile literature. | Plastic scrap—Environmental aspects—Juvenile
literature. | Waste disposal in the ocean—Juvenile literature.
Classification: LCC GC1090 (ebook) | LCC GC1090 .B87 2018 (print) | DDC 363.738—dc23
LC record available at https://lccn.loc.gov/2017037868

Printed in Canada.
010798S18

TABLEOFCONTENTS

ChapterOne: A Surprise at Sea..........................4

ChapterTwo: Shaping a Modern Life....................14

ChapterThree: Risky Ocean Journeys 26

ChapterFour: New Cycles 44

Timeline 56

Glossary 60

Additional Resources 61

Source Notes 62

Select Bibliography 63

Index 64

ChapterOne
A SURPRISE AT SEA

Captain Charles Moore felt the wind across the north Pacific Ocean die to a whisper. A few weeks earlier, it had filled the sails of the *Alguita*, pushing the white 50-foot-long (15-meter-long) sailboat west from California to Hawaii in the 1997 TransPacific Yacht Race. He carried a trophy for third place and was enjoying brisk winds pushing him and his crew back home to California—until now. Moore had scanned weather reports and turned the *Alguita*'s bow southeast. It had entered an expanse of ocean that was as still as a painting.

Sailors usually try to avoid the north Pacific Ocean. The weather there is not too stormy or unpredictable, but too calm. Legends tell of desperate sailors waiting so long for wind that they had to conserve drinking water by drowning their cargo of livestock. Sailors and scientists now understand that this quiet expanse of ocean is the center of a gyre (pronounced JI-er), a whirlpool that is thousands of miles wide. Powerful currents flow around the outer edges, like rivers through the ocean. Driven by the wind and Earth's rotation, the currents sweep west across the Pacific Ocean and up the coast of Asia. Then they move east across the ocean, down the west coast of North America, and west to begin the cycle again.

Captain Charles Moore and his research sailboat, the *Alguita*

The water encircled by the currents turns clockwise sluggishly. Moore's modern sailboat was equipped with diesel engines, a system to make seawater drinkable, and a radio to call for help.

Even so, a detour across these calm waters would haunt him. It would convince him that the ocean held a danger so great that it threatened the survival not only of his crew, but of organisms all over the globe.

On August 8, while standing on deck, Moore saw something unexpected. "Here and there, odd bits and flakes speckle the ocean's surface," he later wrote in the book *Plastic Ocean: How a Sea Captain's Chance Discovery Launched a Determined Quest to Save the Oceans.* He was disturbed because the objects were plastic. He said it looked as if "a giant salt shaker has sprinkled bits of plastic onto the surface of the ocean." Each day he scanned the water and found that "No matter the time of day or how many times a day I look, it's never more than a few minutes before I sight a plastic morsel bobbing by. A bottle here, a bottle cap there, scraps of plastic film, fragments of rope or fishing net, broken-down bits of former things." For seven days the *Alguita* traveled more than a thousand miles with Moore noticing that "They were always there: plastic shards, fluttering like lost moths in the surface waters of the deep, remote ocean."

Moore returned to Alamitos Bay, California, where he had spent his youth swimming, surfing, and sailing in the Pacific Ocean. By the 1980s, he wrote, pollution of many kinds made residents "think twice about eating a fish they caught off the pier."

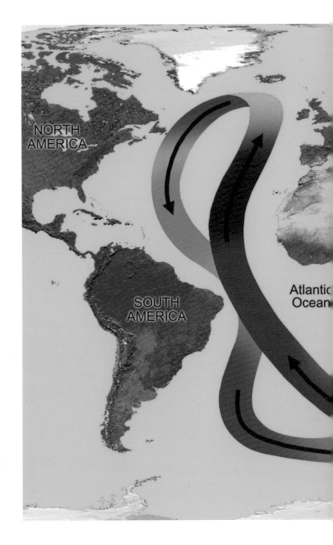

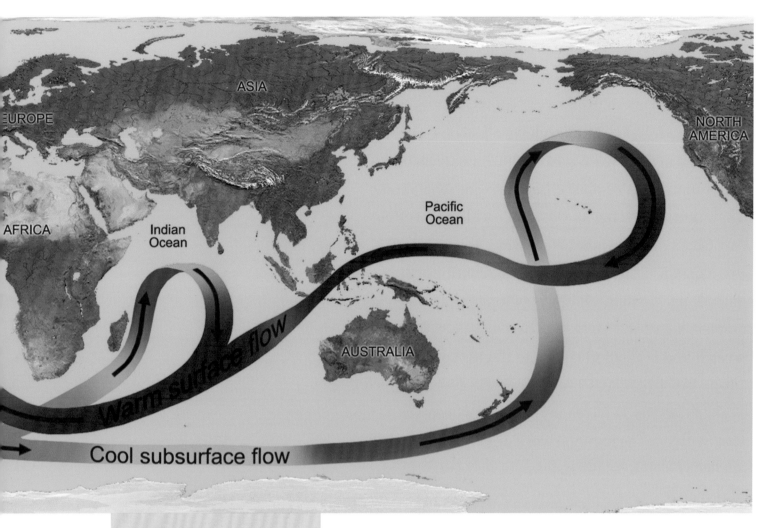

ASIA

EUROPE

NORTH AMERICA

Pacific Ocean

AFRICA

Indian Ocean

Warm surface flow

AUSTRALIA

Cool subsurface flow

A National Aeronautics and Space Administration map of ocean currents depicts warm surface currents in red and deep ocean currents in blue.

Now he wrote that he could not "stop thinking about all those miles and days of plastic. Over the decades we'd gotten used to the sight of trash on the beach, by the roadsides, and in riverbeds, of shopping bags fluttering on fences and branches. … But something seemed very wrong about this plastic trash in the mid-Pacific." He wanted to know why it was there.

Oceanographer Curtis Ebbesmeyer offered Moore an explanation. Since the 1990s Ebbesmeyer had studied how plastic trash moves through the ocean.

He depended on a network of volunteers to report what trash washed up on shores. When containers of manufactured goods slipped off ships, Ebbesmeyer mapped the travels of their buoyant plastic contents to beaches around the world. In 1992 an accidental spill of thousands of plastic bath toys into the Pacific Ocean sent yellow ducks washing up along the U.S. West Coast and Hawaii. "We always knew that this gyre existed," Ebbesmeyer said. "But until the ducks came along, we didn't know how long it took to complete a circuit." For more than a decade, ducks traveled and landed on shores in South America, Europe, Australia, and even the Arctic. Ebbesmeyer realized that the 11 gyres in the world's oceans, along with ocean currents, work together like a giant conveyor belt, circulating seawater and everything floating in it.

Ebbesmeyer convinced Moore that a gyre's slow-moving water does not simply carry plastic bits of trash—it creates them. First a gyre's currents work with a "toilet bowl effect of dragging the debris from the rim and bringing it into the center," Moore said. "But it never flushes. It just keeps adding and adding." In this trash vortex, plastic trash remains trapped for years. Under the sun's ultraviolet rays, plastic turns pale and brittle. It breaks apart in the salty water as waves jostle it endlessly. Gyres slowly shred plastic into bits called microplastics. More than 90 percent of

A PORTRAIT OF PLASTIC

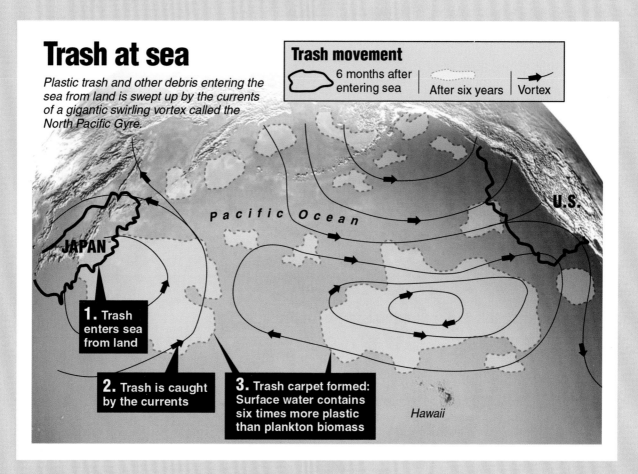

Trash at sea

Plastic trash and other debris entering the sea from land is swept up by the currents of a gigantic swirling vortex called the North Pacific Gyre.

Trash movement

6 months after entering sea | After six years | Vortex

Pacific Ocean

U.S.

JAPAN

1. Trash enters sea from land

2. Trash is caught by the currents

3. Trash carpet formed: Surface water contains six times more plastic than plankton biomass

Hawaii

Currents and gyres circulate water and plastics around the world's oceans.

Plastic trash in the North Pacific gyre is now visible from space. While surveying the zone from an aircraft, researcher Boyan Slat was dismayed to see "debris everywhere. Every half second you see something ... [It] was impossible to record everything. It was bizarre to see that much garbage in what should be pristine ocean."

But locating the nearly invisible microplastics in the ocean takes computer modeling software and a lot of patience. Researchers sail into gyres with nets, called trawls, that drag behind their boats. The nets skim the surface, collecting microplastics. Researchers count the microplastics caught in the tiny mesh with the help of tweezers and sometimes with a microscope. Computer technicians combine new data and thousands of measurements of microplastics collected since the 1970s with information about currents to create maps of where microplastics could be floating.

But the maps are only guesses. Vast parts of the ocean have not been sampled, especially in the Southern Hemisphere. What's more, floating plastic accounts for only 1 percent of the plastic that enters oceans, so much of plastic's ocean journey remains a mystery. "We must learn more about the pathway and ultimate fate of the 'missing' plastic," said marine ecologist Andres Cozar Cabañas.

the plastic at sea might be smaller than a grain of rice. Ebbesmeyer has estimated that a 1-liter plastic bottle crumbles into enough microplastic pieces to put one on every square mile of the world's beaches.

Moore was restless, not for more racing trophies, but for answers. He always had been. In 1994 he had founded the Algalita Marine Research Foundation, an organization to help clean up polluted coastal water. When he helped design the *Alguita*, he equipped the sailboat with a laboratory to analyze water samples. Armed with nets, he and a small crew sailed back to the North Pacific gyre in 1999, searching for what Moore called the "unseen blanket of granular plastics covering the ocean surface" that Ebbesmeyer believed was there.

Some plastic trash was easy to find. Moore observed that "similar objects find each other in the middle of millions of square miles of seemingly empty ocean, and the ocean stitches them together, making a grotesque whole. We dive around this strange mass, avoiding the undulating tendrils of rope and net and deciding it could make a convincing sci-fi monster." Elsewhere in the gyre, they found bobbing bleach bottles, shoes, toothbrushes, bottle caps, sour cream containers, soda bottles, umbrella handles, and soccer balls. Moore knew the gyre would eventually turn this trash into plastic fragments.

The *Alguita* docked in Long Beach, California, for a summit with students and teachers about plastic pollution.

Using fine-meshed nets, Moore's crew skimmed the ocean's surface for nearly 100 miles (161 kilometers). The nets are designed to catch plankton, tiny organisms that provide food for marine animals of all sizes, from sardines to whales. The samples captured in the nets were both "amazing and disturbing," said Moore. "Not one is free of plastic." Plankton formed a jellylike mass, but it was sprinkled with plastic chips. The crew filled 11 jars with samples that resembled "glass snow globes swirling with multicolored plastic snow," Moore wrote.

Moore hauled home barnacle- and algae-covered plastic garbage from the three-week voyage. He displayed it on the *Alguita*'s deck for journalists to photograph. But Moore's attention was on the gyre sample jars headed for the laboratory. "If our results are what we think they'll be, we'll make noise and be heard. Good people will be moved to action," he wrote. Technicians painstakingly separated natural from human-made materials and weighed them. The results were astounding—the microplastics in the samples weighed six times as much as the plankton.

"I wasn't the first to be disturbed about plastic trash in the ocean, and I wasn't the first to study it," said Moore. "But maybe I was the first to freak out about it." He said his new data showed that the debris was "like a ticking time bomb." The data would show people that "their ocean is turning into plastic stew. If they knew, they might begin to see plastics in a new way, maybe handle them more carefully, maybe begin to make different choices." At first scientists were skeptical of studies by this self-taught scientist. But like the wind filling sails, journalists swept the dramatic story into the public eye. A Pulitzer Prize–winning series in the *Los Angeles Times* included Moore's findings in 2006. Headlines called the polluted gyre "the World's Largest Dump." The name "Great Pacific Garbage Patch" caught on.

"I wasn't the first to be disturbed about plastic trash in the ocean, and I wasn't the first to study it. But maybe I was the first to freak out about it."

The microplastics in Moore's samples collected in the Pacific Ocean far outweighed the plankton.

The public did not fully understand what Moore had found. When he described the plastic-stricken area as being twice the size of Texas, people imagined "an island of plastic garbage that you could almost walk on," said Moore's colleague Marcus Eriksen. Moore explained that the gyre is more like "a soup lightly seasoned with plastic flakes, bulked out here and there with 'dumplings': buoys, net clumps, floats, crates ..." People did not fully understand the danger either. "The public sees an island of trash. They picture this giant place that you can go visit," Eriksen said. "It's much worse than that."

ChapterTwo
SHAPING A MODERN LIFE

Charles Moore discovered an unusual rock on Hawaii's Kamilo Beach in 2006. When Canadian geologist Patricia Corcoran heard about it, she flew out to see it. The lump contained shells, coral, wood, and volcanic rock and sand, all fused together by great heat—and plastic. She named it "plastiglomerate" and determined that it had been created by bonfires built by campers on the trash-strewn beach. Corcoran inspected the beach's larger plastic trash and found it had traveled from Russia and Asia, riding a gyre's currents. Colorful microplastics mixed with grains of beach sand—how did they get to this Hawaiian beach so far from the open sea?

Oceanographer Curtis Ebbesmeyer once described how the gyre's polluted center "moves around like a big animal without a leash. When it gets close to an island, the garbage patch barfs, and you get a beach covered with this confetti of plastic." Henderson Island in the south Pacific Ocean, for example, is remote and uninhabited, yet littered with 38 million pieces of plastic.

Like a chunk of plastiglomerate, today's beach sands hold history. "Every little piece of plastic manufactured in the past 50 years that made it into

Beaches littered with plastic and other types of trash are found around the world.

the ocean is still out there somewhere because there is no effective mechanism to break it down," said plastics researcher Anthony Andrady.

Seaglass and bits of ceramic and rusted metal also mix with beach sand to tell an older story. People have always been searching for the best materials to shape into the necessities and luxuries of everyday living. They learned to mold clay, hammer metal, and melt sand into glass. They shaved thin sheets of animal horns to make translucent panes for lanterns. These materials are "plastic" in the sense that they can be easily shaped. The English word plastic comes from the Greek word *plastikos*, which means moldable.

Trees can make a kind of plastic with the help of human creativity. More than 2,000 years ago, the Olmecs, Mayans, and people from other Mesoamerican civilizations cut the bark of rubber trees to release drips of a milky fluid. By mixing in juice from marigold vines, they made rubber elastic and useful for making bouncy balls, stretchy bands, glue, and flexible sandals. Europeans exploring the region in the 16th century were intrigued by this new material and learned how to plant, harvest, and use rubber. By 1830 people living in wet climates eagerly bought rubber-treated clothing and boots invented by Scottish chemist Charles Macintosh. The mackintosh raincoat is named after him but spelled differently.

While rubber was waterproof, it was not weatherproof—in the winter rubber cracked and in the summer it melted. Charles Goodyear, a self-taught American chemist, solved that problem in 1839 after years of tireless experimentation at home, and possibly with the help of an accident. When a lump of rubber mixed with the eggy-smelling chemical sulfur slipped from his hand onto a hot stove, he discovered a transformation—it was dry and firm yet still flexible. This vulcanized rubber, named after Vulcan, the

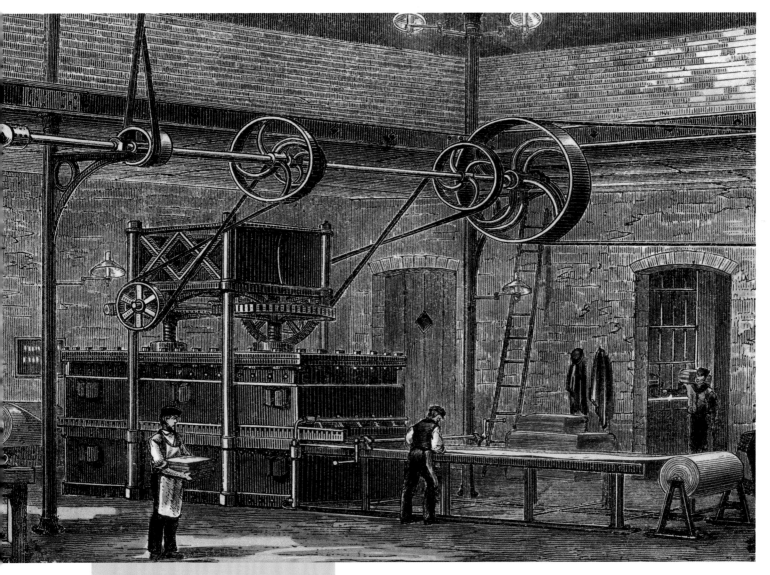

The successful processing of rubber in the mid-1800s led to a wide range of products.

Roman god of fire, now takes many forms, including tires, protective casings for electronic wires, soccer balls, shoe soles, water hoses, and erasers.

A workable recipe for rubber did not end the search for new, multipurpose materials. The urge "to solve problems and to get rich" is strong, Moore pointed out. Natural materials such as tortoiseshell and animal horn, once commonly used to make everyday items like combs, were scarce and expensive. Inventors raced to find ways to manufacture new materials to imitate expensive materials. In the 1860s British chemist Alexander Parkes proved that wood fibers called cellulose could help make more than paper. By adding ingredients such as nitric acid, he created a moldable material for making low-cost everyday items, including combs, buttons, and silverware handles. American factory owner John Wesley Hyatt improved the formula in 1870 and called the new material celluloid. By adding camphor, a waxy chemical, he created a doughy substance that dried hard. He used celluloid to make smooth white billiard balls that looked like expensive elephant ivory and eyeglasses dyed to imitate tortoiseshell. Celluloid was molded, cut, pressed, and polished to make brush handles, piano keys, eyeglass frames, false teeth, and even photographic film.

In the early 1900s, Belgian-American chemist Leo Baekeland recreated a sticky, honey-colored substance produced by Asian beetles. This natural resin coated and protected electrical wires, but it was scarce. Like other inventors, Baekeland turned to natural materials to make a synthetic version. But his raw material—petroleum—originated from ancient plants transformed by pressure and heat deep underground. Despite a laboratory fire, Baekeland experimented with mixing sharp-smelling petroleum gas and liquids derived from coal. Under pressure

DECADES OF EXPERIMENTS

Nature inspired people to make plastics. Natural materials such as rubber, tortoiseshell, cellulose, shellac, wool, cotton, silk, wax, and leather are flexible and durable because of how their molecules fit together. If a molecule can connect in two places to another molecule like itself, the result is called a monomer. When a monomer links with hundreds or thousands of monomers, it forms a long chain-shaped molecule called a polymer. Long polymer chains are the basis of both natural and human-made substances.

Gyres hold the results of decades of experiments with petroleum-based polymers. Scientists adjusted chemicals in hydrogen and carbon chains to create plastics with useful properties. Flexible polyethylene is used to make plastic bags and water bottles. Polypropylene's polymer chains fit closely together and make it heat-resistant for food containers. Scientists added gas to the hydrocarbon chain to create polystyrene, a plastic that can resist impacts, to make computer monitors, furniture, and plastic cutlery. They learned how to make thousands of items, from elastic bubblegum to fishing line to skateboards.

A 1954 ad proclaimed the virtues of laminated plastic panels.

and heat, the result was a thick resin easily poured into molds before it dried hard and glossy. Baekeland named his new material Bakelite, and it has been called the first modern plastic. Advertised as the "material of a thousand uses," it could be molded, drilled, bent, and pressed by machines to create objects of almost any shape. Customers could not get enough of the sleek, fashionable material. It was shaped into doorknobs, toothbrushes, steering wheels, radios, jewelry, pens, telephones, and even coffins. Chemists were soon inventing more petroleum-based materials.

The journey from naturally occurring materials to synthetic ones begins with pumps drawing crude oil from underground. The dark liquid contains many kinds of fuels that must be separated at refineries. Propane is used for furnaces and gas barbecue grills. Gasoline is used for automobile engines. Jet fuel propels planes. About 4 percent of crude oil contains the materials, such as naphtha, that are needed to make plastics. They are heated and mixed with other chemicals to create plastics of various colors and degrees of flexibility, ranging from rigid to rubbery. The new material is extruded into long ribbons, sliced into pellets, and sent to factories. Softened by heat, the raw plastic can take countless forms.

In the 1930s factories puffed up plastic into a light foam for home insulation or stretched it into silky

Crude oil is separated into many kinds of fuels at huge oil refineries.

threads for nylon stockings or toothbrush bristles. Once hand-polished out of tortoiseshell, combs now poured out of plastic factories at the rate of thousands a day. New plastics could take brightly colored dyes or be clear to reveal food inside. Shape-changing was the superpower of a hero in a 1940s comic called *Plastic Man.*

Plastics were enlisted for critical jobs in World War II. They were used to make parachutes and parts for airplanes and guns. They coated antennae and radar cables and lined helmets. Factories manufactured four times as much plastic at the end of the war as they had before the war. After the war factory owners did not want profits to slow. Plastic businesses shifted from supplying soldiers in battle to supplying civilians at home.

Beginning in the 1950s, plastics trickled and then flooded into everyday life, replacing such materials as glass and expensive metals and rubber. Plastic took the shapes of countertops, clear plastic wrap for food, squeeze bottles, electrical plugs, telephones, toothbrushes, and even contact lenses and clear adhesive tape. Children assembled plastic building block sets and played with dolls molded from plastic instead of fragile porcelain. One toy was simply a lump of plastic putty that playful hands could press, pull, and twist into endless shapes. Factories in the 1960s produced stackable chairs molded from a single piece of plastic. Plastics even ventured to the moon in the nylon threads of the flag planted by Neil Armstrong. Later they traveled into the human body with the first artificial heart.

Plentiful and affordable plastics helped shape a new lifestyle. They helped people of all incomes get more for their money. "We were a nation of consumers now, a society increasingly democratized by our shared ability to enjoy the conveniences and comforts of modern life," wrote author Susan Freinkel. Among the modern conveniences and comforts were dishwashers and air conditioners.

Plastics offered another convenience. A 1955 article in *Life* magazine titled "Throwaway Living: Disposable Items Cut Down Household Chores" featured a photograph of a family tossing plates, cups, napkins, and more. "The objects flying through the air would take 40 hours to clean," said the caption, "except that no housewife need bother. They are all meant to be thrown away after use." By the 1960s people were writing with disposable pens instead of refillable fountain pens and drinking coffee from foam cups instead of ceramic ones that required washing.

Yet humans have always found new forms for old materials. Objects made of metal were repaired or the materials used again. Worn-out clothing could be mended, redesigned, or shredded to make paper. But then it sometimes became cheaper to buy new plastic goods than repair old ones. "The idea that you threw stuff out when it wore out is a 20th century idea," wrote Susan Strasser, author of *Waste and Want: A Social History of Trash*.

Plastic trash started accumulating where trash always had, in waterways. From ancient Rome to some cities even today, foul-smelling sewage has polluted drinking water with diseases. Riverside factories have added industrial chemicals. Ohio's Cuyahoga River was so polluted with chemicals that it caught fire in 1969, catching the attention of government leaders.

The federal Clean Water Act added strict rules in 1972 on industrial plants along waterways. But wind and rain sweeps much plastic into waterways from small collections of trash on beaches, roadsides, and

"The idea that you threw stuff out when it wore out is a 20th century idea."

Charles Moore displayed items, including umbrella handles, that had washed ashore on a beach in Hawaii. The trash came from the Pacific gyre.

parks. "Perhaps for a while we weren't as bothered as we might have been," Charles Moore reasoned, "because we still thought plastic material was inert and benign, an eyesore that couldn't do much harm. Now we know better."

ChapterThree
RISKY OCEAN JOURNEYS

The planet Earth, so blue in satellite photographs, is more than 70 percent water. "The oceans seem boundless, like outer space," said Charles Moore. But he and others have seen painful proof that the oceans cannot make all trash disappear. A dead albatross found in 2005 had a piece of plastic inside its stomach from a World War II seaplane that crashed into the Pacific Ocean in 1944. The plastic's 61-year journey likely began with spinning around the North Pacific's second trash vortex near Japan. Then it likely drifted on gyre currents for 6,000 miles (9,656 km) east and spun in the trash vortex Moore discovered—before the albatross mistook it for food. When Moore finds jellyfish embedded with colorful plastics confused for meals, he said he thinks about the truth that "we don't know what it means to weave our artificial plastic materials into the tissue of life." The path of plastic into living bodies is long and well traveled.

Most plastics do not begin their water journey dramatically. They just slip in quietly. Rain overflows dumps and storm drains, carrying trash into rivers. People both ashore and at sea throw trash into the water. About 90 percent of trash entering oceans today is plastic. Five subtropical gyres in the Pacific, Atlantic, and Indian oceans suck in and circulate it slowly

around the world. It takes a decade for a water bottle from California to float to Japan and back. Plastic survives these journeys easily, since it takes 500 years or more to break down.

Visitors to gyres and volunteers cleaning up coastlines find the same type of pollution wherever they go, and much of it is everyday plastic objects used only once. Half of the 600 billion pounds (272 billion kilograms) of plastics manufactured each year become these discarded items. People around the world use a trillion grocery bags a year, but for just 12 minutes on average. In the United States alone, people slurp up drinks using 500 million plastic straws a day. They throw away 2.5 million plastic bottles every hour.

Floating plastics can become traps. Fishers once used nets woven from hemp, cotton, and other natural fibers. Floats made of wood or hollow glass kept nets hanging vertically in the water. Now they can choose plastic foam floats and nylon nets that do not rot, break, or tear easily. The problem is that "a lost nylon fishing net or tangled mass of hook and line does not stop fishing," said Marcus Eriksen, who studies the distribution and impacts of plastic marine pollution. These "ghost nets" drift and trap such animals as dolphins and sea turtles, killing about 1,000 a day. An 11.5 ton (10.4 metric ton) tangle of nets drifting once near Hawaii "looked like a little island of floats" from the surface, said National Oceanic and Atmospheric Administration scientist Mark Manuel. But, he said, it was really a "dark wall of destruction."

Plastic can invite marine animals to take a closer look. While single-use plastic is quickly emptied and discarded, it still looks useful. Hermit crabs move

The stomachs of sperm whales that washed ashore on the North Sea coast in Germany were filled with plastic debris.

into plastic bottle tops instead of shells. Thirteen dead sperm whales washed up on Germany's coast one day in 2016. Researchers discovered the dead whales had eaten unnatural meals of plastic, from fishing line to car parts. Although the litter did not directly cause the whales to beome stranded, it is a concern. Floating plastic bags can look like graceful squid, a popular meal for sperm whales. This tragic mistake "causes them to starve with full stomachs," said conservationist Nicola Hodgins. Sea turtles

Sea turtles, whales, and other sea creatures often mistake floating plastic bags for jellyfish or squid—with deadly results.

mistake plastic bags for a meal of jellyfish. Gases fill their plastic-packed stomachs, making them too buoyant to dive for food or escape predators. A research study indicates that half of the world's sea turtles could contain plastic. Australian scientists estimate that 90 percent of the seabirds that scavenge the ocean's surface have eaten plastic. Researcher Denise Hardesty examined dead seabirds and said, "I have seen everything from cigarette lighters ... to bottle caps to model cars. I've found toys."

But floating plastic makes life easier for some

Invasive zebra mussels cause widespread problems in North America and Europe.

marine animals. Branches, coconuts, and leaves provide rafts for animals that cannot move on their own. Trash provides synthetic rafts that last decades and can cross oceans. A floating buoy or refrigerator door turns into a floating ecosystem when barnacles attach to it. "Like trees in a rainforest," they offer shelter and transportation to coastal creatures such as crabs, said biologist Mike Gil. But globe-traveling organisms are not always welcome. Zebra mussels from the Black Sea hitched a ride on a cargo ship to the Great Lakes in 1988. They multiplied and spread uncontrollably across North America, stealing resources from native species and attaching themselves to water pipes and ship rudders.

Hitchhiking marine life can upset nature's balance in more devastating ways. Under the rotating gyre water, another cycle takes place. Small herbivores called zooplankton eat microscopic, one-celled marine plants called phytoplankton. Small fish, like sardines, eat zooplankton. Larger and faster fish like tuna eat smaller fish. "There's a lot of things there that are hungry all the time," said marine ecologist Miriam Goldstein, who has studied one of those hungry creatures, halobates. The long-legged marine insects skate across the ocean's surface. Normally they stay close to shore and lay eggs on floating pieces of wood or buoyant volcanic rocks. But plentiful microplastics invite them to travel and multiply far beyond their coastal habitats. They feast on zooplankton, which means that sardines may go hungry and that many other larger animals may go hungry too.

Plastic does more than introduce new predators to the gyre. It also becomes a link in the gyre's food chain. Moore once found a 2.5-inch (6.4-cm) fish with 84 plastic pieces inside its belly. Scientists estimate that around 20 percent of fish have eaten plastic. Microplastics, which measure 0.2 inch (5 millimeters)

CHOKING IN THE GYRE

Rescuers saved the life of a plastic-entangled monk seal in Hawaii's waters. Other seals might not be so lucky.

Brightly colored tangles of floating plastic teeming with small animals attract large sea animals. Some of these animals are endangered, like the Hawaiian monk seal photographed by British underwater cameraman Michael Pitts. More than 20 seals a year die after getting tangled in plastic trash. But this one was lucky. Rescuers in Hawaii's Kure Atoll arrived by boat and used a white-handled paddle to hold back the seal's head while cutting away the strangling rope. Scientists are experimenting with designs for biodegradable nets and for devices that use sound to scare large animals away from plastic nets.

About 50 miles (80 km) away, on Midway Island, U.S. photographer Chris Jordan documented other victims of the gyre who were not so lucky. Colorful plastic pieces floating on the ocean surface look like food to a gliding albatross. The birds scoop up seawater, hoping to catch small fish. But often they find plastic and feed it to their chicks, which choke to death. In 2009 Jordan took heartbreaking photographs of their decomposing bodies, revealing plastic chunks of various sizes. "There's a message being sent," he said. "This is the Earth's alarm system going off."

or less, look like inviting zooplankton to hungry fish. This mistake happens again and again because there are more than 5 trillion microplastic pieces drifting at the ocean's surface.

Microplastics are not just found at sea. Snow seemed to coat Hong Kong beaches in 2012, but it was summertime. Millions of pellets of raw plastic had washed up after containers had fallen from a ship. Sunlight weakens plastic trash so it breaks into fragments through photodegradation, but these pea-sized pellets were human-made. Refineries produce these round microplastics, nicknamed nurdles, to sell around the world to manufacturers, which melt them to create plastic products. But nurdles easily escape during transport to bob in the gyre or land on beaches, earning them the gloomy nickname "mermaid's tears." Volunteers in the United Kingdom combed hundreds of beaches and found nurdles on three-quarters of them.

Bathroom sinks offer an unexpected path to the gyre. Until mid-2017, when a U.S. ban took effect, plastic beads smaller than grains of salt were put into toothpaste and facial washes to scrub teeth and skin clean. Every day 8 trillion of the microbeads slipped through drains into U.S. sewage systems, according to researchers at Oregon State University. In underground pipes, the beads joined microplastics escaping homes through wastewater flowing from washing machines.

Clothing made of plastic fibers such as nylon lose fibers less than 0.04 inch (1 mm) long when they are washed. One piece of clothing can release almost 2,000 microfibers. These particles are small enough to slip past filters and race toward streams, rivers, and oceans. They have turned up in table salt in China and in Arctic waters. "I have no doubt that every time I eat oysters and mussels I eat at least one microfiber," said ecology and biology professor Chelsea Rochman. "I see dust in the air and we inhale that. The question is, at what point does it become a problem?"

Microplastics swirling through seawater behave like air pollution. Minute particles from such sources as burning fossil fuels and power plants form a yellow haze over some of the world's cities. They settle in lungs, causing 7 million deaths a year worldwide. Marine life faces a similar threat. "The idea that there are 'patches' of trash in the oceans is a myth," said Eriksen, adding that plastic pollution is more a "'plastic smog,' like massive clouds of microplastics that emanate out of the five subtropical gyres."

Scientists gauging the amount of plastic in gyres have an unusual concern—they are finding too little. About 8 million tons (7.3 million metric tons) of plastic enters oceans each year. Yet samples from shallow regions of the ocean suggest that as little as 40,000 tons (36,300 metric tons) of plastic floats in the ocean. "Ninety-nine percent of our plastic is missing," said oceanographer Erik van Sebille. "We know how much goes in, we know how much is on [the] surface, where's the rest?" The sun, waves, salt, and gyres have done their work well. Most of plastic becomes microplastics. These microplastics have probably already washed up on beaches, sunk to the seafloor, or been eaten.

Scientists in Plymouth, England, worked with a nature film director in 2015 to make a startling video. Viewers saw not a seabird eating a bottle top

"Ninety-nine percent of our plastic is missing. We know how much goes in, we know how much is on [the] surface, where's the rest?"

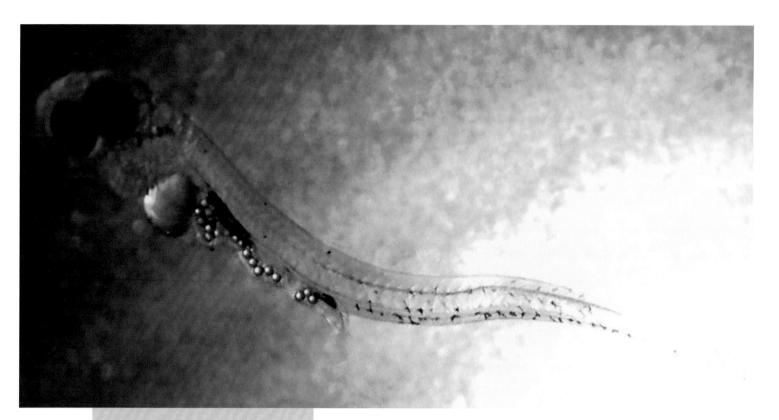

A larval perch ingested microplastic particles as part of a Swedish study on the effects of plastic fragments in waterways.

but zooplankton eating plastic microbeads. Two years later, a video camera equipped with a microscope recorded an arrow worm, a type of zooplankton, ingesting plastic microfibers, which caused a blockage. Once ingested by the tiny, transparent animal, plastic behaves much as a plastic bag does inside a sea turtle. "When I saw it, I thought that here was something, visually, to convey to the public the problem of plastic in the sea," said Richard Kirby, a marine scientist who recorded the 2017 footage. "What intrigues me is that because the fiber has made a loop inside the animal's gut, you can actually see the consequences of something as small as the arrow worm consuming microplastic."

Each time a predator eats prey, plastic travels from one body to the next and forms an expanding collection. Sunlight, salt, and waves cannot dissolve plastic, and neither can stomach acid. That's why the ocean's largest and fastest predators, such as the 100-pound (45-kg) tuna Moore hooked on his 1997 journey through the gyre, can have plastics lodged in muscles and fat that earlier were plankton meals. But plastic's relentless journey does not end at the top of the marine food chain. "There's another top predator in the ocean, it turns out," said marine ecologist Stephen Palumbi. "That top predator, of course, is us." Studies show that microplastics lace one-fourth of the fish sold at seafood markets on both sides of the North Pacific gyre, in Indonesia and California. "What goes into the ocean," said Eriksen, "goes into these animals and onto your dinner plate. It's that simple."

Seafood, whether eaten raw or cooked, delivers many important nutrients to people's bodies. More than 2.5 billion people on Earth depend on seafood for protein. Proteins make up blood, bone, muscle, and brain cells and control the functioning of cells everywhere in the body. But when seasoned with microplastics, seafood can upset a body's delicate balance. The ocean is basically "a toilet bowl for all of our chemical pollutants and waste in general," said Rochman.

From Indonesia to California, people around the world rely on safe fish as part of a healthy diet.

Dangerous chemicals hide inside meals of microplastics. Leaked into oceans through rivers, rainwater, groundwater, and dumping, chemicals attach to tiny plastic rafts for a ride through the world's currents and the food chain. Some of these passengers, molecules of PCBs (polychlorinated biphenyls), were designed to resist high temperatures. Once part of common devices such as industrial equipment, televisions, and refrigerators, they were banned in 1979 because of fear that they cause cancer. Another hitchhiker on microplastics was banned in 1972 for the same reason. DDT, an insecticide, was designed to kill disease-carrying mosquitoes and insects that destroy crops. Like plastics, these chemicals do not dissolve away. The pollutants have been detected in human blood, and PCBs have even been found in shrimplike animals living in the Mariana Trench, 36,000 feet (11,000 meters) below the surface of the Pacific Ocean.

Even without hitchhiking chemicals, microplastics make toxic meals. To add toughness and flexibility, chemicals such as bisphenol A (BPA) and phthalates are added to plastics holding food and drink, such as baby bottles, soda bottles, juice box straws, and food can liners. But these artificial chemicals, when eaten or drunk, confuse some of the body's natural chemicals, called hormones. Hormones carry vital messages ranging from instructions telling the body how to grow and develop to messages that trigger emotions and feelings of hunger. Tests show that BPA levels in U.S. children are twice as high as those of older Americans who grew up with less plastic in their lives.

Plastic that travels back to land as seafood completes an unfortunate cycle. "It's very convenient to roll your trash to the curb every week and have it disappear, but it's a magic trick—and really there's not very much magic," said Edward Humes, who has written a book about the history of garbage. "We need to have less packaging; use less disposable items; [use]

Recyclable items and trash are sorted at a Florida landfill, one of 2,000 landfills in the United States.

things that last longer; make purchasing decisions that are more studied and less wasteful."

In the United States, about half of the nation's trash is buried in landfills, where sturdy liners keep it from having contact with air and nearby soil. Liners also keep trash away from water flowing underground that eventually reaches the ocean. The other half of U.S. trash is recycled or burned to ashes.

But for a third of the people living in the rest of the world, there is no waste management system.

Plastic trash travels wherever wind and water take it. Not far from the western edge of the North Pacific gyre, cockroaches, rats, and goats swarm over a mountain of trash near Jakarta, Indonesia. Every day trucks dump 6,890 tons (6,250 metric tons) more. Thousands of people, including children, live there. They dig through the trash, searching for glass, aluminum, and plastics to sell. They might earn 50 cents a day. No liners contain this growing heap or others in the crowded cities along the gyre.

Cheap, single-use plastic products flood into the Philippines, Vietnam, and Sri Lanka as large businesses based in developed countries collect profits. "It's really about fairness," said environmental activist Matt Prindiville. "If you make something, you need to take responsibility for the environmental and social impacts of that product. When consumer goods companies sell all of their products wrapped in packaging to developing countries that don't have any solid waste or recycling infrastructure, we have rivers of plastic that are literally flowing into the ocean."

Scientists estimate that more than 110 million tons (100 million metric tons) of plastic trash is already in the ocean. By 2050 the plastic in the ocean could weigh more than the fish that live there. "At the end of the day, we have to remember that the ocean is always downstream," said conservation biologist Nicolas Mallos. "It may not reach the ocean today or

Boys searched through the trash on the Indonesian coast.

tomorrow, but we know water flows downstream. We need to think about the items we are using not just on beaches, but also inland and communities far upstream as well."

ChapterFour
NEW CYCLES

Thirteen years after Charles Moore's first voyage to the North Pacific gyre, another catamaran sailed across the same trash vortex. *Plastiki* was built from 12,500 used water bottles. The bottle craft traveled through the gyre not as trash, but as part of a headline-grabbing expedition with a message. "Plastic is not the enemy," said environmentalist and expedition leader David de Rothschild. "But it's our understanding of disposal and reuse that's to blame." Of the 9 billion tons (8 billion metric tons) of plastic produced since 1950, just 2 billion tons (1.8 metric tons) are still in use, a 2017 study found. That means the rest of the plastic litters Earth as trash.

A large study of the Atlantic and Arctic oceans and the Mediterranean Sea in 2014 confirmed that a great deal of this plastic pollution is in the ocean. "This survey has shown that human litter is present in all marine habitats, from beaches to the most remote and deepest parts of the oceans. Most of the deep sea remains unexplored by humans and these are our first visits to many of these sites, but we were shocked to find that our rubbish has got there before us," said marine biologist Kerry Howell of England's Plymouth University.

"This survey has shown that human litter is present in all marine habitats, from beaches to the most remote and deepest parts of the oceans."

Plastiki sailed into Sydney Harbor in Australia after a difficult four-month crossing of the Pacific Ocean. The catamaran faced fierce storms after it left San Francisco, California, in March 2010.

Could a vacuum cleaner suck up the plastic from the ocean surface the way a home vacuum cleans a carpet? Designers of a solar-powered, floating vacuum think so. Others believe ocean currents will naturally push and gather plastic against plastic barriers, where it can be transported to land for recycling. But Australian ecologist Chris Wilcox worries that "it would be as if you were vacuuming your living room, and I'm standing at the doorway with a bag of dust and a fan. You can constantly keep vacuuming, but you could never catch up."

About 80 percent of the ocean's trash comes from land. How can it be prevented from slipping downstream? Scientists turn to nature for ideas. They marvel at nature's efficient system of handling waste. A dead whale or giant redwood tree does not lie on the seafloor or forest floor for centuries. An army of small microscopic organisms turns waste into energy in a form of recycling that means the food chain never ends. These decomposers break dead matter into nutrients and other chemicals, providing food for themselves and plenty to help new grass or phytoplankton grow. Scientists have discovered, often by accident, that among nature's army of decomposers, some can almost miraculously biodegrade plastic. Wax-loving worms enjoy munching on plastic bags. Mealworms willingly feast on plastic foam.

During digestion, these animals secrete enzymes to break down molecular bonds. Even tough plastic water bottles can turn into a meal for bacteria.

Wax worms get their name from the wax they eat in beehives. Scientists discovered that the worms also enjoy eating plastic.

These microbes use enzymes to cut up long polymers into bite-sized sections. Scientists admire how, in a world full of plastics, they have found ways to turn them into food. "If you put a bacteria in a situation where they've only got one food source to consume, over time they will adapt to do that," said microbiologist Enzo Palombo. "I would not be surprised if samples of ocean plastics contained microbes that are happily growing on this material."

Some scientists are not hopeful that biodegradation will solve the plastic problem. They wonder whether worm and bacteria appetites can keep up with the rapid production of plastic.

They also wonder whether people will trust these new waste-removal methods too much. "The public thinks that biodegradability means 'If I throw it away, it will completely go away,'" said biochemistry professor Ramani Narayan. "They don't even know what 'going away' means." Tracy Mincer, who studies plastics in the ocean at the Woods Hole Oceanographic Institution in Massachusetts, said he was impressed with the research on plastic-eating worms but wondered how it will help. "When I think it through, I don't really know where it gets us. I don't see how microbes degrading plastics is any better than putting plastic bottles in a recycling bin so they can be melted down to make new ones."

Simply finding new ways to recycle plastic cannot solve the problem. Even trying to gather and recycle plastic in the gyres "is like mopping up a leaking tap without fixing the tap itself," said oceanographer Erik van Sebille. "It's much better to do it as close to the source as possible, before it has a chance to interact with marine life."

In a grim reminder that plastic is leaking beyond the subtropics, a 2017 study found that microplastics in Arctic waters are a gyre-shredded collection from all over the world. That same year, the United Nations declared war on ocean plastic and asked countries to join the battle against single-use plastics. "It is past time that we tackle the plastic problem that

LIFE CYCLE OF A BOTTLE

Recycling becomes more and more important as the use of plastic grows.

It takes billions of gallons of oil to manufacture all of the plastic water bottles that are used worldwide each year. Yet only about 30 percent of plastic drink bottles are recycled in the U.S. The cost of making plastics that never get recycled means that about $100 billion is lost to the economy each year, according to a World Economic Forum report. "Future populations are going to look at landfills like they are goldmines, full of resources, and wonder what we were all thinking," said Jason Farahnik, project manager at a California recycling facility.

Water bottles to be recycled ride a truck to a sorting facility, where they are sorted into various types of plastic. They travel onward to a recycling facility, where they are washed, sterilized, and ground into small flakes. Some will become new bottles. First they are melted,

extruded like toothpaste, snipped into pellets, and shipped. At manufacturing plants, the pellets are melted, stretched, and blown with air into bottle shapes, and then filled with water again.

A few years ago it seemed that new types of plastics might put traditional recycling plants out of business. Plastic bottles with chemicals added to make them biodegradable arrived in stores along with new plastics made of cornstarch. But in order to biodegrade, these plastics need certain temperatures and exposure to sunlight under tightly controlled conditions. Inside the layers of a landfill or on the seafloor, the new plastics could take as long to break down as the petroleum-based ones. So recycling continues.

A man collected reusable and recyclable items in an Indonesian landfill. As part of the U.N. war on ocean plastic, the country has pledged to dramatically reduce pollution.

blights our oceans. Plastic pollution is surfing onto Indonesian beaches, settling onto the ocean floor at the North Pole, and rising through the food chain onto our dinner tables," said Erik Solheim, U.N. environment director. "We've stood by too long as the problem has gotten worse. It must stop."

Plastic production is expected to double in the next decade and triple by 2050. Every day people fight the war on plastic pollution. They drink from refillable water bottles and take cloth bags to fill at

Volunteers cleaning a beach in Manila in 2014 also sought a ban on plastic bags. Several cities in the Philippines have banned bags, but enforcement is mixed.

the grocery store. Many countries are getting on board by taxing plastic bags to encourage shoppers to use fewer of them. More than 200 U.S. cities have banned plastic bags, and so have such countries as Kenya, China, Rwanda, and France. The U.K., Australia, and Canada are moving toward banning the sale of products containing microbeads. And slowly, campaigns against plastic drinking straws are convincing some restaurants to ban them—or at least to offer one only if a customer requests it.

But what if cleaning up the ocean does not require a war on plastic but rather a war on litter? "All of that stuff was in a human's hand at one point or another," said ecologist Wilcox. "The essence of the solution is to provide incentives for people not to throw this stuff away. It is the cheapest, simplest, and far most efficient solution to the problem."

On a record-breaking solo voyage around the world in 2005, British sailor Ellen MacArthur learned to waste nothing. "Your boat is your entire world, and what you take with you when you leave is all you have. That's food, fuel, clothes, even toilet roll and toothpaste. That's what we do. And when we leave, we manage it down to the last drop of diesel and the last packet of food. No experience in my life could've given me a better understanding of the definition of the word finite. What we have out there is all we have. There is no more," MacArthur said. "Our global economy is no different. It's entirely dependent on finite materials we only have once in the history of humanity." In 2010 she started a foundation to help change attitudes toward waste of many kinds. Like fellow sailor Moore, MacArthur admired the efficiency of nature's cycles. "Life itself has existed for billions of years and has continually adapted to use materials effectively. It's a complex system, but within it, there is no waste," she said.

MacArthur and others who share her ideas believe

Ellen MacArthur at the helm of her boat, nicknamed *Mobi,* during her 2005 solo sail around the world

that people must leave behind the throwaway living habits of the 1950s. Nature offers a solution. Plastic and other nonliving materials can be part of an endless cycle of usefulness, like nature's food chains. In a throwaway culture, plastics travel a straight, quick path from petroleum to raw plastic to useful product to trashcan to landfill to the ocean. With a different approach, plastic could travel a circular path in which it never became waste. "Plastic has become synonymous with cheap and worthless, when in fact those chains of hydrocarbons ought to be regarded as among the most valuable substances on the planet," wrote author Susan Freinkel. Plastic has been celebrated for being adaptable, long-lasting, and lightweight but strong. Finding ways to reuse it will benefit the world and its future generations.

Recycled plastic bags, bottles, and foam packaging can be turned into playground equipment, park benches, clothing, carpeting, and car batteries. Recycled plastic bags can be used to create asphalt for paving city streets. Plastics provide materials for construction, medical equipment, cars, airplanes, 3D printing ink, and spacecraft. "If we could build an economy that would use things rather than use them up, we could build a future that really could work in the long term," said MacArthur. Then plastic would not end up floating uselessly in the ocean.

Geologist Patricia Corcoran wondered whether "in the future, people will find plastiglomerate buried in the soil and realize that it is a permanent symbol of humankind's pollution of our natural world."

Thousands of teachers, schoolchildren, and volunteers cleaned a California beach as part of a campaign to raise awareness of the impact of litter and pollution on the ocean.

She wondered whether the planet will by then be smothered with out-of-control plastic waste. Or will people have solved the problem of plastic pollution? As a start, she said, "we can all pitch in and help through beach cleanups and not using as many plastic products. Maybe by raising awareness [of how serious the problem is], people will start to say, 'OK, that's kind of disgusting so maybe ... I should think twice before I buy a bunch of balloons or use a straw. Even small things make a difference."

Timeline

1823

Scottish inventor Charles Macintosh finds a way to make clothing waterproof by mixing rubber and naphtha, a petroleum product

1839

American inventor Charles Goodyear discovers that adding sulphur to rubber creates weatherproof products; vulcanization made commercial use of rubber possible

1907

American chemist Leo Baekeland develops the first synthetic plastic using petroleum-based ingredients; popular Bakelite products become part of many aspects of daily life

1933

By accident during an experiment, a team of British chemists discovers how to make polyethylene

1856

British chemist Alexander Parkes develops a plastic material from cellulose

1870

John Wesley Hyatt improves Parkes' cellulose-based recipe, adding camphor to produce a plastic that can be shaped and colored

NEW YORK WORLD'S FAIR

19 39

GLASS CENTER BUILDING

1939

Patented in 1935, stockings made of nylon, the first human-made fiber created in a laboratory, debut at the New York World's Fair

1948

The federal Water Pollution Control Act is the first major U.S. law to regulate water pollution

Timeline

1965

Swedish chemists patent a plastic bag; by manufacturing long, flattened tubes, many grocery-style bags can be produced at once by sealing seams and slicing openings

1972

The federal Clean Water Act gives the U.S. Environmental Protection Agency the authority to set safe water quality standards

1989

Oceanographer Robert Day describes plastic pollution in the North Pacific gyre near Japan

1997

Captain Charles Moore discovers a trash vortex in the eastern side of the North Pacific gyre; his study of the area two years later revealed the extent of the pollution

1973

American engineer Nathaniel Wyeth invents the plastic soda bottle using polyethylene terephthalate (PET); the sturdy design can hold the pressure of carbonated beverages

1980

Oceanographer Robert Morris discovers plastic pollution in the South Atlantic Ocean

2016

France is the first country to ban plastic plates, cups, and utensils, passing a law to take effect in 2020

2017

The United Nations launches a Clean Seas campaign to reduce ocean pollution; it calls on individuals and businesses to reconsider the ways waste is produced and handled

Glossary

benign—not harmful

biodegrade—to break down through the work of bacteria and other small organisms

cellulose—substance that makes up the cell walls and fibers of plants

ecosystem—living things and their environments functioning as a unit

emanate—originate from

enzyme— substance produced by a living organism that triggers chemical reactions

extrude—to shape by forcing through an opening

finite—having limits or bounds

hormones—substance produced by a living organism that works like a messenger, telling cells how to behave and controlling such functions as digestion, reproduction, and growth

microbe—microscopic organism that often causes disease or biodegradation

molecule—atoms making up the smallest unit of a substance

plankton—collection of water-dwelling organisms carried by the sea and fresh water

synthetic—artificial, resulting from reactions of artificial chemicals instead of naturally occurring

ultraviolet— form of radiation with waves shorter than those of visible light that can penetrate skin and other surfaces

vortex—mass of swirling liquid, especially a whirlpool, that draws objects to its center

Additional Resources

Further Reading

Kallen, Stuart A. *Trashing the Planet: Examining Our Global Garbage Glut.*
Minneapolis: Twenty-First Century Books, 2017.

Mulder, Michelle. *Trash Talk! Moving Toward a Zero-Waste World.*
Custer, Wash.: Orca Book Publishers, 2015.

Newman, Patricia. *Plastic, Ahoy!: Investigating the Great Pacific Garbage Patch.*
Minneapolis: Millbrook Press, 2014.

Internet Sites

Use FactHound to find Internet sites related to this book.
Visit *www.facthound.com*
Just type in 9780756557454 and go.

Critical Thinking Questions

The polluted area of the North Pacific gyre discovered by Charles Moore has been described by scientists and journalists as a garbage patch, an island, smog, soup, and a vortex. How do these names affect the way people understand marine plastic pollution?

In what ways does plastic pollution affect groups of people around the world? Consider economic and geographic factors.

The Ellen MacArthur Foundation advocates using and reusing resources in a circular economy as opposed to the current system of making, using, and disposing of items. A circular economy would keep items in use for as long as possible and then reuse materials. What examples of a circular economy for plastic have you seen in your life, at home, at school, or around your hometown?

Source Notes

Page 6, line 6: Charles Moore and Cassandra Phillips. *Plastic Ocean: How a Sea Captain's Chance Discovery Launched a Determined Quest to Save the Oceans.* New York: Avery, 2011, p. 3.

Page 6, line 11: "Garbage Mass is Growing in the Pacific." *The Bryant Park Project.* NPR. 26 March 2008. 22 Sept. 2017. http://www.npr.org/templates/story/story.php?storyId=89099470

Page 6, line 14: *Plastic Ocean: How a Sea Captain's Chance Discovery Launched a Determined Quest to Save the Oceans,* p. 3.

Page 6, line 21: Ibid.

Page 6, line 27: Ibid., p. 7.

Page 7, line 1: Ibid., p.17.

Page 8, line 8: Richard Fisher. "How Lego figures and rubber ducks reveal ocean secrets." BBC. 22 July 2014. 22 Sept. 2017. http://www.bbc.com/future/story/20140722-odd-objects-reveal-ocean-secrets

Page 8, line 21: Spencer Miles. "World's Oceans Face Problem of Plastic Pollution." *PBS Newshour.* PBS. 13 Nov. 2008. 22 Sept. 2017.http://www.pbs.org/newshour/bb/environment-july-dec08-plasticocean_11-13/

Page 8, line 23: "Garbage Mass is Growing in the Pacific."

Page 9, col. 1, line 3: Oliver Milman. "'Great Pacific garbage patch' far bigger than imagined, aerial survey shows." *The Guardian.* 4 Oct. 2016. 22 Sept. 2017. https://www.theguardian.com/environment/2016/oct/04/great-pacific-garbage-patch-ocean-plastic-trash

Page 9, col. 2, line 10: Laura Parker. "First of Its Kind Map Reveals Extent of Ocean Plastic." *National Geographic.* 16 July 2014. 22 Sept. 2017. http://news.nationalgeographic.com/news/2014/07/140715-ocean-plastic-debris-trash-pacific-garbage-patch/

Page 10, line 13: *Plastic Ocean: How a Sea Captain's Chance Discovery Launched a Determined Quest to Save the Oceans,* p. 56.

Page 10, line 17: Ibid., p. 83.

Page 11, line 6: Ibid., p. 82.

Page 11, line 9: Ibid., p. 109.

Page 12, line 5: Ibid., p. 111.

Page 12, line 12: Ibid., p.124.

Page 12, line 16: Ibid., p. 152.

Page 13, line 4: Asia-Pacific Correspondent, Daniel Howden, and Kathy Marks. "The world's rubbish dump: a tip that stretches from Hawaii to Japan." *The Independent.* 5 Feb. 2008. 20 Sept. 2017. http://www.independent.co.uk/environment/green-living/the-worlds-rubbish-dump-a-tip-that-stretches-from-hawaii-to-japan-778016.html

Page 13, line 6: *Plastic Ocean: How a Sea Captain's Chance Discovery Launched a Determined Quest to Save the Oceans,* p. 4.

Page 13, line 10: Katherine Martinko. "'The Smog of the Sea' is Jack Johnson's new film about plastic pollution." Treehugger. 14 Feb. 2017. 22 Sept. 2017. https://www.treehugger.com/ocean-conservation/smog-sea-jack-johnsons-new-film-about-plastic-pollution.html

Page 14, line 16: Kenneth R. Weiss. "Altered Oceans. Part Four: Plague of Plastic Chokes the Seas." *Los Angeles Times.* 2 Aug. 2006. 22 Sept. 2017. http://www.latimes.com/world/la-me-ocean2aug02-story.html

Page 14, line 24: Ibid.

Page 17, line 6: *Plastic Ocean: How a Sea Captain's Chance Discovery Launched a Determined Quest to Save the Oceans,* p. 24.

Page 20, line 5: Jeffrey L. Meikle. *American Plastic: A Cultural History.* New Brunswick, N.J.: Rutgers University Press, 1995, p. 1.

Page 22, line 23: Susan Freinkel. "A Brief History of Plastic's Conquest of the World." *Scientific American.* 29 May 2011. 22 Sept. 2017. https://www.scientificamerican.com/article/a-brief-history-of-plastic-world-conquest/

Page 23, line 5: Ben Cosgrove. "'Throwaway Living': When Tossing Out Everything Was All the Rage." *Time.* 15 May 2014. 22 Sept. 2017. http://time.com/3879873/throwaway-living-when-tossing-it-all-was-all-the-rage/

Page 24, line 13: Olivia B. Waxman. "The History of Recycling in America Is More Complicated Than You May Think." *Time.* 15 Nov. 2016. 22 Sept. 2017. http://time.com/4568234/history-origins-recycling/

Page 25, line 1: *Plastic Ocean: How a Sea Captain's Chance Discovery Launched a Determined Quest to Save the Oceans,* p. 73.

Page 26, line 2: Ibid., p. 59.

Page 26, line 15: Charles Moore. Email interview. 23 Sept. 2017.

Page 28, line 15: Marcus Eriksen. "Impacts of Plastic Pollution on Marine Life." EcoWatch. 1 Aug. 2014. 22 Sept. 2017. https://www.ecowatch.com/impacts-of-plastic-pollution-on-marine-life-1881940409.html

Page 28, line 22: Eve Conant. "Hunting for 11-Ton Fishing Net in the War Against Ocean Trash." *National Geographic.* 8 June 2015. 22 Sept. 2017. http://news.nationalgeographic.com/2015/06/150608-ocean-trash-hawaii-endangered-species-marine-science-fishing/

Page 28, line 25: Ibid.

Page 29, line 9: Philip Hoare. "Whales are starving—their stomachs full of our plastic waste." *The Guardian.* 30 March 2016. 22 Sept. 2017. https://www.theguardian.com/commentisfree/2016/mar/30/plastic-debris-killing-sperm-whales

Page 30, line 9: The Associated Press. "Up to 90% of seabirds have plastic in their guts, study finds." *The Guardian.* 31 Aug. 2015. 22 Sept. 2017. https://www.theguardian.com/environment/2015/sep/01/up-to-90-of-seabirds-have-plastic-in-their-guts-study-finds

Page 31, line 6: Elizabeth Preston. "Barnacles Plus Plastic Trash Make Rafts for Ocean Animals." *Discover.* 22 Feb. 2016. 22 Sept. 2017. http://blogs.discovermagazine.com/inkfish/2016/02/22/barnacles-plus-plastic-trash-make-rafts-for-ocean-animals/#.WR9ZttKGPIU

Page 32, line 11: Daniel Strain. "Ocean Trash Is a Lifesaver for Insect." *Science.* 8 May 2012. 22 Sept. 2017. http://www.sciencemag.org/news/2012/05/ocean-trash-lifesaver-insect

Page 33, col. 2, line 9: Chris Jordan. "Midway Journey." TEDxRainier. 7 Jan. 2012. 22 Sept. 2017. https://www.youtube.com/watch?v=MjK0cvbm20M 8:20

Page 35, line 24: Jessica Boddy. "Are We Eating Our Fleece Jackets? Microfibers Are Migrating Into Field and Food." *The Salt: What's On Your Plate.* NPR. 6 Feb. 2017. 22 Sept. 2017. http://www.npr.org/sections/thesalt/2017/02/06/511843443/are-we-eating-our-fleece-jackets-microfibers-are-migrating-into-field-and-food

Page 36, line 7: Marcus Eriksen. "Plastic Smog: Microplastics Invade Our Ocean." EcoWatch. 27 Feb. 2015. 22 Sept. 2017. https://www.ecowatch.com/plastic-smog-microplastics-invade-our-oceans-1882013762.html

Page 36, line 18: "A Sea of Plastic: How scientists and entrepreneurs are tackling the growing problem of our ocean's trash." *Popular Science.* 26 Sept. 2016. 22 Sept. 2017. http://www.popsci.com/sea-plastic

Page 37, line 7: Mark Kinver. "Video captures moment plastic enters food chain." BBC News. 11 March 2017. 22 Sept. 2017. http://www.bbc.com/news/science-environment-39217985

Page 38, line 10: Stephen Palumbi. "Hidden toxins in the fish we eat." TED Talks. April 2010. 22 Sept. 2017. https://www.ted.com/talks/stephen_palumbi_following_the_mercury_trail/transcript?language=en

Page 38, line 16: "The world's rubbish dump: a tip that stretches from Hawaii to Japan."

Page 38, line 26: Eliza Barclay. "How Plastic in the Ocean Is Contaminating Your Seafood." *The Salt: What's On Your Plate.* NPR. 13 Dec. 2013. 22 Sept. 2017. http://www.npr.org/sections/thesalt/2013/12/12/250438904/how-plastic-in-the-ocean-is-contaminating-your-seafood

Page 40, line 23: Thelma Gutierrez and George Webster. "Trash city: Inside America's largest landfill site." CNN. 28 April 2012. 22 Sept. 2017. http://edition.cnn.com/2012/04/26/us/la-trash-puente-landfill/

Page 42, line 14: "'The Smog of the Sea' is Jack Johnson's new film about plastic pollution."

Page 42, line 25: Laylan Connelly. "Thousands turn out to rid coast of trash." *The Orange County Register.* 21 Sept. 2013. 22 Sept. 2017. http://www.ocregister.com/2013/09/21/thousands-turn-out-to-rid-coast-of-trash/

Page 44, line 7: Brian Handwerk. "Plastic Bottle Catamaran Completes Epic Pacific Crossing." *National Geographic.* 28 July 2010. 22 Sept. 2017. http://news.nationalgeographic.com/news/2010/07/100727-plastc-bottle-catamaran-completes-epic-pacific-crossing/

Page 44, line 18: Jessica Aldred. "Human litter found in Europe's deepest ocean depths." *The Guardian.* 30 April 2014. 22 Sept. 2017. https://www.theguardian.com/environment/2014/apr/30/human-litter-european-seafloor-survey-ocean-deep

Page 46, line 5: Laura Parker. "The Best Way to Deal With Ocean Trash." *National Geographic.* 16 April 2014. 22 Sept. 2017. http://news.nationalgeographic.com/news/2014/04/140414-ocean-garbage-patch-plastic-pacific-debris/

Page 47, line 4: Karl Mathiesen. "Could a new plastic-eating bacteria help combat this pollution scourge?" *The Guardian.* 10 March 2016. 22 Sept. 2017. https://www.theguardian.com/environment/2016/mar/10/could-a-new-plastic-eating-bacteria-help-combat-this-pollution-scourge

Page 48, line 2: Dave Gilson. "Do Biodegradable Plastics Really Work?" *Mother Jones.* May/June 2009. 22 Sept. 2017. http://www.motherjones.com/environment/2009/04/do-biodegradable-plastics-really-work/

Page 48, line 10: Deborah Netburn. "These newly discovered bacteria can eat plastic bottles." *Los Angeles Times.* 10 March 2016. 22 Sept. 2017. http://www.latimes.com/science/sciencenow/la-sci-sn-bacteria-eat-plastic-20160310-story.html

Page 48, line 17: "A Sea of Plastic: How scientists and entrepreneurs are tackling the growing problem of our ocean's trash."

Page 48, line 27: "UN Declares War on Ocean Plastic." UN Environment. 5 March 2017. 22 Sept. 2017. http://www.unep.org/gpa/news/un-declares-war-ocean-plastic

Page 49, col. 1, line 7: Debra Winter. "The Violent Afterlife of a Recycled Plastic Bottle." *The Atlantic.* 4 Dec. 2015. 22 Sept. 2017. https://www.theatlantic.com/technology/archive/2015/12/what-actually-happens-to-a-recycled-plastic-bottle/418326/

Page 52, line 2: "The Best Way to Deal With Ocean Trash."

Page 52, line 10: Ellen MacArthur. "The surprising thing I learned sailing solo around the world." TED Talks. March 2015. 22 Sept. 2017. https://www.ted.com/talks/dame_ellen_macarthur_the_surprising_thing_i_learned_sailing_solo_around_the_world/transcript?language=en

Page 52, line 24: Ibid.

Page 54, line 6: Susan Freinkel. "Plastic: Too Good to Throw Away." *The New York Times.* 17 March 2011. 22 Sept. 2017. http://www.nytimes.com/2011/03/18/opinion/18freinkel.html?mcubz=0

Page 54, line 20: "The surprising thing I learned sailing solo around the world."

Page 54, line 26: Patricia Corcoran. Email interview. 12 June 2017.

Page 55, line 4: Carla Herreria. "Plastiglomerate: The New and Horrible Way Humans Are Leaving Their Mark On the Planet." *HuffPost.* 19 June 2014. 22 Sept. 2017. http://www.huffingtonpost.com/2014/06/19/plastiglomerate_n_5496062.html

Select Bibliography

"Captain Charles Moore … Talks Trash." Conversation. *Earth Island Journal*. Spring 2009. 22 Sept. 2017. http://www.earthisland.org/journal/index.php/eij/article/charles_moore/

Cho, Renee. "Our Oceans: A Plastic Soup." State of the Planet. Earth Institute. Columbia University. 26 Jan. 2011. 22 Sept. 2017. http://blogs.ei.columbia.edu/2011/01/26/our-oceans-a-plastic-soup/

Ellen MacArthur Foundation. 22 Sept. 2017. https://www.ellenmacarthurfoundation.org/

Eriksen, Marcus. "Microbeads and the Plastic Smog: How We're Saving Our Seas." *HuffPost*. 1 June 2016. 22 Sept. 2017. http://www.huffingtonpost.com/marcus-eriksen/microbeads-and-the-plastic-smog_b_7484110.html

Fears, Darryl. "There's literally a ton of plastic garbage for every person on Earth." *The Washington Post*. 19 July 2017. 22 Sept. 2017. https://www.washingtonpost.com/news/energy-environment/wp/2017/07/19/theres-literally-a-ton-of-plastic-garbage-for-every-person-in-the-world/?utm_term=.3b58271fb98d&wpisrc=nl_energy202&wpmk=1&wpmm=1

Griswold, Eliza. "How 'Silent Spring' Ignited the Environmental Movement." *The New York Times*. 21 Sept. 2012. 22 Sept. 2017. http://www.nytimes.com/2012/09/23/magazine/how-silent-spring-ignited-the-environmental-movement.html?mcubz=0

Harp, Stephen L. *A World History of Rubber: Empire, Industry, and the Everyday*. Malden, Mass.: Wiley Blackwell, 2016.

Hodal, Kate. "Living off the landfill: Indonesia's resident scavengers." *The Guardian*. 27 Sept. 2011. 22 Sept. 2017. https://www.theguardian.com/world/2011/sep/27/indonesia-waste-tip-scavengers

Knight, Laurence. "A brief history of plastics, natural and synthetic." BBC News. 17 May 2014. 22 Sept. 2017. http://www.bbc.com/news/magazine-27442625

Kostigen, Thomas M. "The World's Largest Dump: The Great Pacific Garbage Patch." *Discover*. 10 July 2008. 22 Sept. 2017. http://discovermagazine.com/2008/jul/10-the-worlds-largest-dump

Leeson, Craig, director. *A Plastic Ocean*. Plastic Oceans Ltd. 2016.

Meikle, Jeffrey L. *American Plastic: A Cultural History*. New Brunswick, N.J.: Rutgers University Press, 1995.

"Midway—Island of Life." Michael Pitts. Underwater Cameraman. 22 Sept. 2017. http://www.michaelpitts.co.uk/movies.php?m=12

Milman, Oliver. "US to ban soaps and other products containting microbeads." *The Guardian*. 8 Dec. 2015. 22 Sept. 2017. https://www.theguardian.com/us-news/2015/dec/08/us-to-ban-soaps-other-products-containing-microbeads

Moore, Charles, and Cassandra Phillips. *Plastic Ocean: How a Sea Captain's Chance Discovery Launched a Determined Quest to Save the Oceans*. New York: Avery, 2011.

More Ocean Less Plastic. The 5 Gyres Institute. 22 Sept. 2017. https://www.5gyres.org/videos/

Nelson, Bryan. "What can 28,000 rubber duckies lost at sea teach us about our oceans?" Mother Nature Network. 1 March 2011. 22 Sept. 2017. http://www.mnn.com/earth-matters/wilderness-resources/stories/what-can-28000-rubber-duckies-lost-at-sea-teach-us-about

Poole, Steven. "Following the jetsam." *The Guardian*. 22 May 2009. 22 Sept. 2017. https://www.theguardian.com/books/2009/may/23/flotsametrics-curtis-ebbesmeyer-scigliano

Schlossberg, Tatiana. "Trillions of Plastic Bits, Swept Up by Current, Are Littering Arctic Waters." *The New York Times*. 19 April 2017. 22 Sept. 2017. https://www.nytimes.com/2017/04/19/climate/arctic-plastics-pollution.html

"Special Report: Altered Oceans." *Los Angeles Times*. July/August 2006. 22 Sept. 2017. http://www.latimes.com/world/la-fg-altered-oceans-sg-20060730-storygallery.html

"Throwaway Living: Disposable Items Cut Down Household Chores." *Life*, p. 43. 1 Aug 1955. 22 Sept. 2017. https://books.google.com/books?id=xlYEAAAAMBAJ&printsec=frontcover&source=gbs_ge_summary_r&cad=0#v=onepage&q&f=false

United Nations Environment Programme. "The Clean Seas global campaign on marine litter." The Ocean Conference. June 2017. 22 Sept. 2017. https://oceanconference.un.org/commitments/?id=13900

Wanucha, Genevieve. "A Quarter Million Tons of Plastic Float in Our Oceans, says Dr. Marcus Eriksen." Oceans at MIT. 10 Dec. 2014. 22 Sept. 2017. http://oceans.mit.edu/news/featured-stories/269000-tons-plastic-ocean-now-dr-marcus-eriksen

Wilcox, Christie. "Five Trillion Pieces of Plastic Are Floating in an Ocean Near You." *Popular Science*. 19 May 2015. 22 Sept. 2017. http://www.popsci.com/five-trillion-pieces-plastic-are-floating-ocean-near-you-3

World Economic Forum. "The New Plastic Economy: Rethinking the future of plastics." 19 Jan. 2016. 22 Sept. 2017. http://www3.weforum.org/docs/WEF_The_New_Plastics_Economy.pdf

Index

Algalita Marine Research Foundation, 10
Alguita sailboat, 4–5, 6, 10, 12
Andrady, Anthony, 15
Armstrong, Neil, 22

Baekeland, Leo, 18, 20, 56
Bakelite, 20, 56
beaches, 8, 14, 15, 34, 35, 55
biodegradation, 33, 46–47, 49
birds, 26, 30, 33, 36

celluloid, 18, 57
chemicals, 24, 39–40
cleanup, 45–46, 52, 55
Clean Water Act (1972), 24, 58
conservation, 50–51, 55, 57, 59
consumption, 28, 29, 30, 32, 36–38
Corcoran, Patricia, 14, 54–55
Cozar Cabañas, Andres, 9
crabs, 28–29, 31
currents, 4–5, 8, 9, 14, 26, 27, 39, 46

Day, Robert, 58
DDT, 39–40
de Rothschild, David, 44

Ebbesmeyer, Curtis, 7–8, 10, 14
Eriksen, Marcus, 13, 28, 36, 38
experiments, 16, 18, 19, 33, 56

Farahnik, Jason, 49
fish, 6, 26, 28–29, 32, 38, 42
fishing industry, 28
Freinkel, Susan, 22, 54

Gil, Mike, 31
Goldstein, Miriam, 32
Goodyear, Charles, 16, 56
gyres, 4, 8, 9, 14, 19, 26–27, 32, 33, 36, 48

halobates, 32
Hardesty, Denise, 30
Hodgins, Nicola, 29
hormones, 40

Howell, Kerry, 44
Humes, Edward, 40–41
Hyatt, John Wesley, 18, 57
hydrocarbons, 19, 54

Jordan, Chris, 33

Kirby, Richard, 37

landfills, 41, 49
Life magazine, 23–24

MacArthur, Ellen, 52, 54
Macintosh, Charles, 16, 56
Mallos, Nicolas, 42–43
Manuel, Mark, 28
microplastics, 8, 9, 10, 12, 14, 32, 34–36, 38–40, 48
Mincer, Tracy, 48
monomers, 19
Moore, Charles, 4, 5–7, 8, 10–13, 14, 17, 25, 26, 32, 38, 58
Morris, Robert, 59

Narayan, Ramani, 48
nets, 9, 10, 11, 28, 33
North Pacific gyre, 9, 10–11, 12–13, 38, 42, 44, 58
nurdles, 35
nylon, 21, 22, 28, 35, 57

oil, 20, 49

Palombo, Enzo, 47
Palumbi, Stephen, 38
Parkes, Alexander, 18, 57
petroleum, 18, 19, 20, 49, 54, 56
photodegradation, 34
phytoplankton, 32, 46
plankton, 11, 12, 38
plastic bags, 19, 28, 29–30, 37, 46, 51, 54, 58
plastiglomerate, 14, 54
Plastiki catamaran, 44
polyethylene, 19, 56, 59
polymers, 19, 47
polypropylene, 19
polystyrene, 19

Prindiville, Matt, 42
products, 20, 21, 35, 39, 40–41, 42, 51, 55, 56

recycling, 41, 42, 46, 48, 49, 54
Rochman, Chelsea, 35, 38
rubber, 16–17, 19, 22, 56

seafood, 38, 40
seals, 33
sea turtles, 28, 29–30, 37
Slat, Boyan, 9
Strasser, Susan, 24

throwaway culture, 53–54
trawls, 9

van Sebille, Erik, 36, 48

Water Pollution Control Act (1948), 57
whales, 11, 29, 46
Wilcox, Chris, 46, 52
World War II, 21–22, 26
worms, 37, 46–47, 48
Wyeth, Nathaniel, 59

zebra mussels, 31–32
zooplankton, 32, 34, 37

About the Author

A former teacher, Danielle Smith-Llera taught children to think and write about literature before writing books for them herself. As the spouse of a diplomat, she enjoys living in both Washington, D.C., and overseas in countries such as India, Jamaica, and Romania.